PAST & PRESENT

CAMPBELL COUNTY

OPPOSITE: When one's name is Gillette, they are automatically associated with the Gillette razor company. Advertisements called Gillette "Razor City" and, like the sign shown here, "The Sharpest Town in the West." Just to set the story straight, the city of Gillette is not related to the division of Procter & Gamble that makes razors. (Courtesy of the City of Gillette.)

PAST & PRESENT

CAMPBELL COUNTY

Mary Kelley with photographs from the Campbell County Rockpile Museum

This book is dedicated to the Campbell County Rockpile Museum, Board, and Association. They have encouraged me and supported me by allowing the use of their photographs, experiences, and knowledge in writing my three books with Arcadia Publishing. I could not have done this without them.

ISBN 978-1-4671-0640-5

Library of Congress Control Number: 2020947752

Published by Arcadia Publishing
Charleston, South Carolina

Printed in the United States of America

For all general information, please contact Arcadia Publishing:
Telephone 843-853-2070
Fax 843-853-0044
E-mail sales@arcadiapublishing.com
For customer service and orders:
Toll-Free 1-888-313-2665

Visit us on the Internet at www.arcadiapublishing.com

On the Front Cover: In 1902, W.A. "Al" Dodd bought two lots on Gillette Avenue and built the Dodd House, a hotel, restaurant, and bar, shown in the past picture. In 1905, Sam and Maggie Goings bought the hotel and renamed it the Goings. In 1937, Phil Chapman bought the hotel, tore down the original frame building, and erected the current brick structure. The current owners, Rick and Becky Eischeid, remodeled the entire building, inside and out, in 2015. (Past, courtesy of the Campbell County Rockpile Museum; present, by Mary Kelley.)

On the Back Cover: This is an older image of the wooden suspension bridge that spanned the fishing lake at Dalbey Park, named for former mayor "Peanuts" Dalbey. The old bridge was built in 1964 and reconstructed in 1988. Lots of Campbell County adults remember playing on the bridge and scaring their siblings by making the bridge swing. (Courtesy of the Campbell County Rockpile Museum.)

Contents

Acknowledgments

We are truly blessed that the Campbell County Rockpile Museum has such an extensive database of photographs. Its board and staff actively pursue additional historic photographs from this area to round out its collection. They understand that photographs taken "yesterday" are also historical and can be of great value to record what is happening now. In fact, some of the past photographs in this book I took less than 25 years ago when I first moved here. Gillette and Campbell County have changed so much in the last two decades that it is fun to compare pictures taken so recently with the same scene today. A huge thank you goes to everyone at the Rockpile Museum for their help sending me sample photographs, finding the images I needed, scanning, copying, and just being supportive.

Two other organizations need to be mentioned. One is the *Gillette News Record* and its predecessors, the journalists who wrote the stories and ran the ads that were everyday news but offer so much historical information today. The other organization is the Campbell County Public Library, whose staff has created binders filled with those stories and ads from the newspapers. The binders are by year with indices, and each article has the date it originally ran written on it. The binders are invaluable to a researcher on a time schedule.

I also received photographs from Tami Erb at First Interstate Bank; Luke Bennett at Accent Masonry; the City of Gillette; Terry Brown at Boothill Steakhouse & Nightclub; Reece Vissia at Bruce Dees & Associates, LLC; Eric Perez at Belle Ayr Mine; Peabody Powder River Mining, LLC (Rawhide Mine); West Texas Trail Museum in Moorcroft; and the Wright Centennial Museum. All past photographs are courtesy of the Campbell County Rockpile Museum unless otherwise noted. All present photographs are by Mary Kelley unless otherwise noted.

Introduction

There are many reasons why people came to the area that is now northeastern Wyoming. To the Native Americans, it was part of the Dakota Territory, sacred land not to be infringed upon. To early explorers like John Jacob Astor and Wilson Price Hunt, it was a brief stop on their way to Oregon. To the Chicago, Burlington & Quincy Railroad, it was one stop on the railroad tracks as they continued to Alaska. To homesteaders, it was free land from the government. Whatever the reason they were here, these early visitors and residents did not create crowded cities and major thoroughfares. It seems the people who settled in northeastern Wyoming and stayed wanted few neighbors, less government, and a slower lifestyle. The pull of the wide-open spaces and independent way of life is as strong today as it was 200 years ago.

Explorers, trappers, and homesteaders camped on Donkey Creek in the late 1800s and called their little tent town Donkey Town. The rail line being constructed through northeast Wyoming was originally to follow Donkey Creek. Edward Gillette, a surveyor with the railroad, saved the company money by changing the route of the tracks, which resulted in naming the new little town after him. The town of Gillette was platted in 1891, and lots sold for $1.25 per acre. Gillette was a true Western town with cowboys, rodeos, shootings, and lots of saloons. The town stayed very small, but ambitious settlers applied for homesteads in the surrounding areas, creating ranches out of the prairie. Many homesteaders gave up on the land with very little rain and lots of wind, but some stayed and have celebrated centennial ranch status. For many years, Gillette was a busy livestock loading stop on the railroad. Cattle and sheep shared the range, not without a few disputes.

For settlers who wanted even more distance from their neighbors, small communities sprang up around Gillette. Wright, Rozet, Recluse, and Spotted Horse could be considered suburbs if you use that term loosely. Wright is the only incorporated town among those four. It was planned as a community for coal miners who worked at the mines in the southern part of the county. The name "Wright" honors the family of the same name who once owned that land.

On the Great Plains, where timber is scarce, alternative fuels were necessary for heating homes. Fortunately, settlers found ample supplies of coal just below the surface. Anyone with a pick and shovel could dig a winter's worth of coal from a nearby hillside. In the 1970s, that coal would change the face of not only Campbell County but also the state of Wyoming and the country. The Powder River Basin—where Campbell County is located—became the largest producer of sub-bituminous coal in the United States. Not only is Campbell County blessed with coal, it is also rich in natural gas, uranium, and rare earth minerals. These riches allow residents to enjoy first-rate schools, infrastructure, amenities, and a comfortable lifestyle. However, legislative regulations have changed the future of coal to the extent the economy in Campbell County has been threatened. The silver lining to this threat is that innovation and diversification may just save the day and the county.

Gillette and Wright have experienced booms and busts during their growth years, resulting in committed, dedicated residents who can handle anything. People are quick to help each other in times of need. For a community with many transients, there is a family feel to the area. One of my favorite things about Campbell County is that many pioneer families who settled this area are still here. Countless family names in this book are still prominent families who are even now contributing to the quality of life in Campbell County. Gillette could have stayed in the 20th century with metal buildings and no attention to beauty or recreation, but visionaries sometimes made unpopular decisions to offer residents and visitors aesthetics and plenty to do. Gillette and Wright both offer sculptures, flower planters, parks, and playgrounds. Nearby are mountains to climb, places to hunt and fish, and state-of-the-art recreational facilities. As seen in the present pictures, Campbell County rivals any similar size community in beauty and modern amenities.

CHAPTER 1

A Great Place to Live

This simple photograph is the perfect representation of life on the Great Plains in 1924. Three unidentified people sit on Black Butte just south of Gillette, not far from their home in the distance. Hardy homestead families who toughed it out in the early years were rewarded with coal, oil, and gas discovered on their property.

For 36 years, the Campbell County Recreation Center was located on the Douglas Highway. As early as 2005, the Campbell County Parks and Recreation Department knew the facility was too small for the growing community. A much larger recreation center opened in 2010 on Enzi Drive. The current photograph shows Legacy Living and Rehabilitation Center, where the old recreation center used to be. This long- and short-term care facility features amenities like a theater and bistro and overlooks Lasting Legacy Park. (Past, courtesy of the City of Gillette.)

One of the popular features of the Campbell County Recreation Center in the mid-1970s was the winding slide splashing into the swimming pool. By the early 1980s, the Campbell County Parks and Recreation Department added a new running track, basketball and racquetball courts, and many new programs. Today, the parking lot for Legacy Living and Rehabilitation Center has replaced the space vacated by the old pool. The Legacy is a part of Campbell County Health's system of care facilities.

Campbell County acquired the 12-acre site at Eighth Street and Douglas Highway in 1990 and razed the old armory to make room for a new park. A citizen group named it Lasting Legacy Park for Gillette's centennial. The park was built in phases as funds were available and includes an amphitheater, playground, picnic tables, and sculptures. A huge need at the time was for more soccer fields and volleyball courts, so those were also included. (Past, courtesy of the City of Gillette.)

Built in 1917 by the Gilstrap family, the Isis Theater was the place for plays, musicals, and eventually, moving pictures, allowing the people of Gillette to see Charlie Chaplin and Buster Keaton in early silent films. The building has housed many businesses over the years, from the Gillette Motor Company to a printing shop to Graham Motors and a thrift store. The building was torn down in October 2017 to make way for additional parking for First Northern Bank.

A free movie starring Bob Hope and Rhonda Fleming marked the grand opening of the Sky-Hi I Drive-In theater on June 27, 1963. For 39 years, residents enjoyed movie entertainment under the stars while children amused themselves on the playground equipment and bought treats at the concession stand. In 1975, Sky-Hi II and III indoor theaters opened near the entrance to the drive-in. Now all three theaters are gone, replaced by a residential neighborhood.

The older picture shows the wooden suspension bridge that spanned the fishing lake at Dalbey Park, named for former mayor "Peanuts" Dalbey. The old bridge was built in 1964 and reconstructed in 1988. Lots of Campbell County adults remember playing on the bridge and scaring their siblings by making the bridge swing. The new bridge was renovated in 2020 and does not swing. Imagine Dalbey Park if park planners had not planted hundreds of trees in the early years.

At first glance, these two photographs look the same. However, the past photograph features the Gillette Golf Club on the land in front of the Gillette–Campbell County Airport. When airport expansion was considered in the growth years of the 1970s, there was no room to keep the golf course in that location. The present photograph still reflects the buttes and hills of the Great Plains but shows the manicured look of the present-day airport.

Campbell County's fairgrounds were once located on Second Street, just east of the Rockpile to Richards Street. From modest beginnings, the fairgrounds grew to include grandstands, shown in the past photograph, exhibit buildings, and barns for livestock. When Cam-Plex Multi-Event Facilities were built in the 1980s, the county fair moved to those facilities. The county fair celebrated 100 years in 2020. Today, that space includes Campbell County Fire Station No. 1 and several buildings belonging to the Campbell County government.

The ground was broken on June 15, 1982, for the Campbell County Senior Center shown in the past photograph. It was a welcome milestone for the seniors who had met in church basements and at the Campbell County Recreation Center but just needed a place of their own. Seniors enjoyed daily lunches and activities but soon outgrew the original building. In 2009, work began on a $7-plus-million expansion, providing space to serve 400 at meals, office space, and activity rooms.

The first games at the new baseball field north of the railroad tracks were played in 1968 by the American Legion baseball team under coach Bill Kennedy. Since 1968, many improvements have been made to the field, including turf, bleachers, and outfield fencing. The past picture shows one of the major improvements, an indoor practice facility, erected in 2009. In the present picture, the Volunteer Field House proudly displays sponsors who keep Legion baseball going under coach Nate Perleberg.

Built in 1972 as the Elks lodge, Boothill quickly became a popular hangout once it became a bar, restaurant, and meeting place. The building has changed owners several times but has primarily kept the Boothill name. Owner Terry Brown purchased the property in 2013 and quickly painted over the turquoise exterior and added lodgepole decor for a true Western look. (Past, courtesy of Terry Brown.)

The Energy Capital Sports Complex, also known as "Field of Dreams," adds tremendously to the quality of life. Built in 2015, the complex includes four diamonds that can be used by Little League or ladies' fast-pitch softball. The city bought 320 acres at Boxelder and Garner Lake Roads to be developed as recreational site in 2011. The preliminary master plan included additional ballfields, an aquatic center, an accessible playground, a covered stadium, and a toboggan run, as funds allow. (Past, courtesy of Bruce Dees & Associates, LLC.)

McDonald's, the largest fast-food chain in the world, has two locations in Gillette. The first, shown in the past picture, was built in 1978 on Camel Drive near the Campbell County High School. Owner Larry Storo bought his first McDonald's in Sheridan in 1968 and owns five McDonald's as of 2020. The original Gillette McDonald's was razed and rebuilt in early 2019, shown in the present picture. The second location, at Skyline Drive and Westover Road, opened in 2013. (Past, courtesy of the City of Gillette.)

CHAPTER 2

A County Grows Out of the Prairie

Nothing shows growth more than a "Welcome" sign at the entrance to the city with the population listed. In 1935, Gillette's population was 1,500, and Wright was not an incorporated town yet. The year 2020 is a census year, so the current population is unknown but estimated to be approximately 35,000. Population for the entire county is estimated at 45,000.

Gillette and Wright are the only two incorporated towns in Campbell County. In 1977, when this past photograph of Boxelder Road looking east from 4-J Road was taken, Gillette's population was approximately 14,000, and Wright would not be officially dedicated until 1978. Campbell County had begun a boom period starting with the opening of several surface coal mines. The tax benefits of millions of tons of coal sales allowed Gillette to pave roads like Boxelder Road in the present photograph. (Past, courtesy of the City of Gillette.)

Provident Federal Savings & Loan, Wyoming's oldest federally chartered savings and loan association, announced the grand opening of its Gillette branch in November 1976. The bank featured in the past photograph was built at Sixth Street and Douglas Highway. Before the building was completed, it operated out of a mobile facility across the street starting in April 1975. This bank was also named Metropolitan Federal Bank, First Bank, and currently, US Bank. (Past, courtesy of the City of Gillette.)

Wyoming National Bank, in the past picture, opened in Gillette in 1975, but from 1985 to 1988, Norwest operated the bank as a franchise. This photograph is dated August 1977. The Gillette branch location of Wells Fargo was established on October 18, 1974, during one of the most significant boom periods in Campbell County. (Past, courtesy of the City of Gillette.)

The 1970s were a time of huge growth for Campbell County. To accommodate the increasing population, retail stores like Buttrey Foods opened in Gillette, as seen in the past picture. Prior to the coal boom, smaller grocery stores like Red Owl, McClelland's, and Lindsey's provided the needs of the residents. In 1998, Smith's Food & Drug Centers bought 13 existing grocery stores, including the Gillette store shown in the present picture. (Past, courtesy of the City of Gillette.)

Adequate housing has often been a problem in both Gillette and Wright. Indian Hills apartments, patio homes, and townhouses opened in 1975, designed in clusters to devote more space to recreation and open areas. Carter Mining Company, Atlantic Richfield Company, Sun Oil, Pacific Power & Light, and Amax Coal Company were involved in this project to provide homes for their employees. Today, Indian Hills homes and apartments stay full by offering many amenities at an affordable price. (Past, courtesy of the City of Gillette.)

This rendering shows the Holiday Inn under construction in August 1977. The new facility included a swimming pool, restaurant, and banquet facilities for groups up to 500 people. The hotel was built as a "Holidome," popular in the 1970s, with an indoor waterpark. The feature many people remember is the glass slide onto the glass dance floor. This hotel has had many names over the years, including Thunder Basin Holiday Hotel, Clarion Hotel and Convention Center, and currently, Ramada.

The Sands Restaurant and Lounge was a popular gathering spot in Gillette from 1961 to 1986. The Sands was built by brothers John and Bob Ostlund, plus James Daly, Quentin Marquis, and Quentin's wife, Toots. They brought big-name entertainment to Gillette, including the Ink Spots and the Jimmy Dorsey Band. In 1963, the Sands Motor Lodge was added. The restaurant was torn down in 1989 to make way for Hardee's. The motor lodge is currently Alamo Inn & Suites.

Gillette's mayor Mike Enzi, chamber of commerce officials, and Kmart dignitaries attended Kmart's grand opening on November 16, 1978. New residents may not know this was the first location of Kmart on North US Highway 14-16, not the second location on Douglas Highway. When Kmart moved from this location to Douglas Highway in 1991, Casper Movie Palace bought the Kmart building but not to install a theater, since Foothills Theater was right next door. The Kmart building was transformed into retail.

From Pamida to Freeds to Mossholders to Lerwick's to Conlin's, this much-used building was finally demolished in May 2012. That same year, Campbell County approved an expansion to the Children's Developmental Services building that was located in front of the Conlin's building. The expansion doubled the space available for children as the center matches children with disabilities in its classes with an equal number of non-disabled children. For many years, there is a waiting list.

The Farmer's Marketing Union was formed by a handful of ranchers here in the 1930s or 1940s to sell their grain in bulk in Omaha, where they could make twice the money they were offered here for it. Sometime in those early years, the name changed to Farmer's Cooperative Association. The gas station in the past picture was built in 1940 at Second Street and Brooks Avenue. In 2020, Enterprise Rent-a-Car occupies that space.

The early 2000s were growth years in Campbell County, with new neighborhoods popping up, especially south of Gillette. In 2001, residential areas preceded business growth. In the past photograph, the view southeast from the Southpark subdivision shows nothing south of the former Campbell County South Campus, shown to the far left. The present picture shows the current Thunder Basin High School on the far left plus the school's soccer field, running track, and football stadium, as well as a neighborhood playground.

Looking north from the Southpark subdivision, also in 2001, the neighborhood was still being finished. In the distance, the pink Christinck house and outbuildings are still standing, and one can see into the Sutherland subdivision across old 4-J Road. Nineteen years later, that same view is blocked by additional housing in Southpark, mature trees, and landscaping. Neighborhoods like Remington Village, RC Ranch, and College Park have added to the growth on the south side of Gillette.

Growth in the retail sector was a source of great excitement for the residents. Every new store was welcomed by enthusiastic shoppers who did not have to drive several hours to visit a similar store elsewhere. In 2012, the Powder Basin Shopping Center stayed pretty full of tenants. An additional building had to be constructed to accommodate Jo-Ann Fabrics and Crafts in November 2012. Other businesses built during this boom included Petco and Sports Authority, both located in the same shopping center.

William Wintermute Sr. was the owner of the Almo Truck Stop in 1953 when it was built at Second Street and Burma Avenue. Placemats in the onsite café boasted "sleeping accommodations for tired drivers." In 1958, Almo became the Husky Super Stop gas station, keeping the same manager, Loren Kemp. Vic Toscana is the owner of the Thunder Basin Ford dealership, shown in the present photograph.

High-paying jobs at the newly opened coal mines attracted many new residents. The population boom happened so fast in the 1970s that Campbell County could not build infrastructure fast enough. Tent cities and recreational vehicle (RV) parks sprang up to accommodate the need. Gypsy Will's RV park was one place where "dogs, kids and long-hairs are allowed." In 1978, Wyoming Machinery Company opened at this location as a Caterpillar dealer, serving the coal mines and oil and gas industries. (Past, courtesy of the City of Gillette.)

CHAPTER 3

RICHES FROM THE LAND

At the time of this photograph in 1946, Wyodak Mine had been operating for 23 years. At one time, Wyodak was considered the largest seam of coal in the world. This wall of coal is approximately 100 feet deep. Wyodak was the first coal mine in the Powder River Basin to use conveyors to move coal to the plant.

Among the laws passed by the Wyoming Legislature in 1919 was an appropriation of $15,000 for an experimental farm in Campbell County. The J.R. Cates land east of Gillette was purchased for $25 per acre. The purpose of the farm was to determine what crops are best suited to this environment. Some of the crops planted include oats, wheat, potatoes, and sunflowers. In 1984, the farm was purchased by Campbell County to add to Cam-Plex acreage. (Past, courtesy of the City of Gillette.)

Burlington Lake was created by the Burlington Northern Railroad Company to provide water for steam engines coming through Gillette as well as the residents of the city. Livestock and horses were watered at the lake in the early 1900s, and children learned to swim in this lake. The lake was dredged several times to allow it to hold more water. The lake is now a habitat for waterfowl and includes an island designated for bird migration and walking paths.

The first George Keeline died in 1900 at 75 years after a successful career as a landowner, banker, and financier. In his will, he declared no sheep would be run by the family firm. However, several years later, his descendants decided sheep were a good investment and added thousands to their holdings. Wool warehouses by the railroad tracks were necessary. In the 1980s, the warehouses were demolished to make way for other railroad buildings or parking.

Back in 1928, Ben Powell built and financed the first elevator at First Street and Carey Street. That elevator lasted until 1961, when it was torn down, and the present one was built in its place. The Sheridan Flour Mill elevator was purchased and used as the west elevator. A feed mill was added in 1971 but has been removed to allow for fence panel inventory, shown in the present photograph. Be prepared for the remaining elevator to be removed soon.

Belle Ayr Mine, shown in the past picture, was the first commercial coal mine to open in the Powder River Basin since Wyodak Mine. It opened in 1972, and soon a dozen more coal mines opened, leading to a huge economic boom in Campbell County. Before mining begins, each company has to create an environmental impact statement and reclamation plan. The present picture shows that same pit after mining and responsible reclamation are complete. (Past, courtesy of the City of Gillette; present, courtesy of Eric Perez, Belle Ayr Mine, Eagle Specialty Materials, LLC.)

Construction began on Rawhide Mine in September 1974. The mine opened in 1976, with production beginning in August 1977. When it opened, Rawhide was owned by the Carter Mining Company. Currently, the mine is owned by Peabody Powder River Mining, LLC, and is located about 10 miles north of Gillette. In its early years, Rawhide had three silos. In the present picture, the mine features six silos. (Present, courtesy of Peabody Powder River Mining, LLC.)

The Neil Simpson Unit No. 2 is a coal-fired power plant, part of the Neil Simpson Complex along with Wygen Units 1 and 2. All of these plants use coal from the nearby Wyodak Mine. Wyodak Mine is operated by Wyodak Resources Development, a subsidiary of Black Hills Corporation. Neil Simpson Unit No. 2 generates 90 megawatts of energy. Each megawatt of a coal power station's capacity can supply 650 average homes. The ground breaking for Neil Simpson Unit No. 2 occurred in 1993.

Former Wyoming governor Dave Freudenthal participated in the 2007 ground breaking for the Dry Fork Station. Dry Fork Station burns coal from Dry Fork Mine, approximately one mile east. Dry Fork Station is the newest coal-fired plant in the country as well as a hub for carbon emissions research and innovation. The Integrated Test Center is located at the station, where researchers develop ways to capture carbon dioxide from power plants and make valuable products with it.

Westside Elementary School became the Alternative Transitional Center and then became Westwood High School. In August 2014, a new Westwood High School opened on the Gillette Campus, behind the Technical Education Center. After the old Westwood was demolished, Matt Walker started Equality State Farms, LLC, an urban farm business, and planted crops on the old Westwood site plus three other sites. The business came about because of the coronavirus pandemic, a time when products like food were hard to find.

CHAPTER 4

The Suburbs

Freda Pringle, a resident of the little town of Spotted Horse, Wyoming, in the 1920s, sits on the steps of the post office, filling station, and country store. The town was named for a Native American chief once prominent in that area. Spotted Horse is 37 miles from Gillette on US Highway 14-16.

The current bar was constructed after a fire destroyed the original building around 1935. The bar included a store and post office. The horse in the past photograph was a two-dimensional wooden cutout covered with genuine spotted horsehide. The horse in the present photograph is a three-dimensional, life-size horse called "Old Spot," photographed thousands of times by tourists. There was also a dance hall just east of the store that was destroyed by a tornado in 1944.

Before Interstate 90 was built across Wyoming, Spotted Horse was a thriving community, complete with a school and quite a few residents. But once the interstate was built, life bypassed the community, and today, only the bar and an abandoned school building are left. The original school is shown in the past picture in the mid-1920s. As the population grew, another small schoolhouse was brought to this location and joined with the original building to accommodate all the students.

Established in 1914, the Recluse Post Office was named for an abandoned post office in South Dakota. The Oedekoven family was responsible for the post office and attached store from 1924, when Fred Oedekoven was appointed postmaster. Fred set up the post office in a small building adjacent to the existing store. In the present photograph, the sign for the store and post office is still there, but the buildings are home to more Oedekovens.

Gillette was originally part of Crook County until 1911, when the state created Campbell County. Before 1911, Moorcroft and Gillette were in the same county. Many of the founding families lived in Moorcroft at that time and just happened to homestead east of what would be the county line. Downtown Moorcroft is shown in the past picture in 1936 and in 2020 in the present picture. Hopper's Bar is the only business on the left side remaining from 1936.

The town of Wright is Gillette's closest incorporated neighbor, 45 miles southwest. The town is named for the Wright family, who lived in this huge house on the corner of Gillette Avenue and Fourth Street. Bill Wright was mayor of Gillette and a representative in the legislature and served on many local boards. The big house is no longer here, having been replaced by the Village Square Mall in 1980.

The Wright Centennial Museum opened in July 1990 on the same day the Cowboy State celebrated its centennial; however, Wright had a long history before that. A post office was established in Wright in 1906 and continued until 1942, when it closed. With the advent of the many coal mines nearby, the old Wright charter was reactivated in 1976, and the town was incorporated in 1985. The original museum was pretty small, but a large building was added in 2012.

In the past picture, Cottonwood Elementary School in Wright is almost finished in December 1979 after two years of construction. The school was modeled after Wagonwheel Elementary in Gillette as far as having many open classrooms. When it opened in early 1980, Cottonwood housed 217 students in grades one through eight and 12 teachers, plus principal Delmer Blankenhagen and his staff. The other picture shows the school today, with 206 students, 13 teachers, principal Derek Barnhurst, and staff.

CHAPTER 5

Essential Services

Clark Reynolds and Charley Fieldgrove purchased this hearse in 1980, when it was about 75 years old. Fieldgrove said when he drove the hearse hooked up to his Belgian team, "it rode as smooth as a Cadillac." This photograph shows the hearse taking Charley Fieldgrove to his final resting place at Mount Pisgah Cemetery in December 1985.

As Gillette grew, St. Matthew's Catholic Church outgrew its walls downtown and relocated to Butler-Spaeth Road on Gillette's east side. Butler-Spaeth Road was named for early pioneers George Butler and Ernest Spaeth. It is thought the very first house in Campbell County was on the Spaeth ranch. The past picture shows Butler-Spaeth Road in November 1977 and the Catholic church on the right. In the present picture, one can barely see the church on the right for all the trees. (Past, courtesy of the City of Gillette.)

The entrance to Mount Pisgah Cemetery in Gillette in 1971 is substantially different from the current entrance. A Campbell County cemetery district was passed in 1964, which allowed for tax funds to be collected to maintain and improve all the cemeteries in the district. There are currently nine cemeteries in the district. Pisgah is a Biblical name meaning "high place," like the top of a mountain. Mount Pisgah Cemetery is situated on one of the highest spots in Gillette.

Carl Joseph Cook was buried temporarily in Flanders Field in Belgium after he died on July 15, 1918, in World War I. In 1921, his body was shipped home for a grand burial at Mount Pisgah, attended by hundreds of mourners. Two years later, it was learned that Cook's body was actually discovered in another battlefield grave and sent home for its rightful burial in Gillette. Notice the huge difference in landscaping and esthetics from the 1920s to today.

The flagpole for many years was at the top of the hill at Mount Pisgah. It was moved to its present location in about 1950. It is at its present location that the local veterans' organizations celebrate Memorial Day and Veterans Day. The present picture is an excellent reflection of the increase in trees, paved roads, and landscaping that make the cemetery a beautiful and peaceful resting place.

Inspiration Gardens, at the top of Mount Pisgah Cemetery, began as a dream in 2010 for the cemetery trustees who wanted to extend the life of the cemetery. By removing 320 available burial plots, they created 3,382 urn chambers and 24 burial spots when the gardens were complete. A three-season shelter has been built at Inspiration Gardens and is available for events, including weddings. A similar spot, Unity Garden, is located along East Eighth Street. (Past, courtesy of Luke Bennett, Accent Masonry.)

The First Baptist Church is the oldest church in Gillette. Before the building was erected in 1902, church services were held at the old city hall or at a ranch. The church was built at 306 Kendrick Avenue and was the only church in Gillette until 1906, when the Catholic church was built. The original church was sold in 1963 and removed in 1973. The present picture shows the area behind Gillette's central shopping district where the original church stood.

St. Matthew's Catholic Church moved from downtown Gillette to the east side in 1976. The parish hall, built in 1962, remained on Gillette Avenue, purchased by the Campbell County School District and used for various activities. As the parish hall, it contained a large gymnasium, classrooms, a kitchen, and two upstairs apartments. Due to structural concerns, it was demolished in the summer of 2019, with the resulting space finished as additional parking for Twin Spruce Junior High.

Tiggie Hines was one of the oldest members of the Church of the Holy Trinity Episcopal, and it was through her efforts and those of some fellow Episcopalians that this church was built in Gillette in 1912. The parsonage next door was built in 1916. The bell and its tower were torn down in 1945 during a remodel, and the bell was stored at the old Saunders Lumber Company, unbeknownst to the congregation, until it was discovered 52 years later.

Early in the 1920s, Effie Rooney took in women to care for while awaiting the birth of a child as well as "unfortunates" who had no one to care for them. Dr. J.C. McHenry persuaded the Rooneys to remodel their building to include an operating room and all necessary equipment to make it a first-class hospital. The Rooney Hospital became the McHenry Hospital when Dr. McHenry bought the building at 103 Kendrick Avenue. Today, there is nothing left of the building.

This house at 202 Warren Avenue looks almost identical today to how it looked in the 1940s, when it was the Gillette Hospital. The third floor was the nursery, with several rooms for male patients. The second floor contained six to eight rooms for surgical patients. The first floor was where recovering patients stayed as well as the kitchen. Most recently, the building has been divided into apartments.

Before the current Campbell County Health hospital was built, and after the much smaller Rooney Hospital and Gillette Hospital, a one-story Campbell County Memorial Hospital was built. It was a 39-bed hospital that opened in 1953, shortly after the death of Dr. McHenry. The five-acre site, formerly part of the old Civilian Conservation Corps (CCC) camp, was donated by Roy, Lloyd, and William Underwood. The early hospital building has been replaced by the Campbell County Senior Center, an essential service.

The past picture records the footings being poured for the original part of the "new" Campbell County Memorial Hospital in November 1977. The construction was completed in 1981, eighteen months behind schedule. Twenty-seven patients were moved from the old hospital on Eighth Street in just one and one-half hours in February. All 55 beds in the new facility were ready for use when the doors officially opened at noon on February 14, 1981, the same time the old hospital closed. (Past, courtesy of the City of Gillette.)

Wyoming has long been thought to be a drive state, meaning most people travel by car to visit. That is certainly true of tourists, but corporate travelers need the speed and efficiency of air travel. The old Campbell County Airport Terminal served the public as well as private pilots for many years. When the new terminal was built in 1997, the old terminal was limited to private pilots, flying lessons, and other services not offered by the major airlines.

CHAPTER 6

EDUCATIONAL OPPORTUNITIES

Floyd and Emily (Colgate) Robinson had nine children, six of whom are shown here on their horse in front of Spring Creek Elementary School in 1932. The boys, from left to right, are Jean, Jess, Don, Colgate, John, and Floyd. The Robinson family lived on a homestead on Spring Creek in southern Campbell County until 1939, when the property was sold to Floyd Reno and the family moved to Montana.

The Bundy School was named for S.L. Bundy, on whose homestead the school was located. This typical one-room schoolhouse was 14 feet by 22 feet. After 70 years, the school closed in 1986, and students were sent to the new 4-J School. The Bundy School was sold to Dan McBeth and moved to his ranch. The old McKay School was also moved to that location; both buildings were remodeled into a home and are now on private property.

The old school in the past picture was built as a high school in 1912 in the third block of Kendrick Avenue. In 1924, it became a grade school when the high school moved to Seventh Street and Gillette Avenue, now Twin Spruce Junior High School. In 1935, the school district discontinued using the old building, but the county did use it for offices for a while. The building was torn down in 1960, and the post office was built there in 1976. (Past, courtesy of Randy Thomas.)

On the east side of Rozet Elementary School stands the original 5,000-square-foot gymnasium built by the Works Progress Administration in 1935. In 1983, a second gymnasium was built to allow students to eat lunch in the new gym while physical education classes were conducted in the old gym. The lava rock was a cheaper material than any other. The old gym is still in use today, but part of its unique facade is blocked by storage buildings.

The first Rozet schoolhouse was built in 1917, a one-room building west of the current school. A high school was added in 1919. Note the covered wagons on either side of the school in the past photograph. Those were the school buses in the early days. The first school was where Ruff's Rozet Bar is today, shown in the present picture. Meet some long-term Rozet ranchers: from left to right, Aldin Reynolds, Chuck Reynolds, John Fowler, Mary Knigge, Gary Thar, and John Reynolds. (Past, courtesy of Wyoming State Archives, SCH140.)

The site of the old Stocktrail Elementary School became the site of the new Stocktrail after a ground breaking in May 2015. Van Ewing Construction was awarded the bid on the $17-million school scheduled to open in the fall of 2016. The two-story design is unique in Campbell County, and Stocktrail is also the first elementary to offer a dual-language immersion program. Students study math, science, language arts, and social studies in Spanish for half a day and English for the other half.

This football field belonged to the Campbell County High School when this photograph was taken on June 5, 1938. Looking north toward downtown Gillette, Kendrick Avenue is seen extending from the north end of the field. The high school is on the left side, and Mount Pisgah Cemetery is on the far right. The current football field belongs to Twin Spruce Junior High, now in the location of the old high school.

Although a second high school campus had been discussed since the 1980s, it was not until 2017 that the Campbell County School District transformed the South Campus into Thunder Basin High School. The South Campus was home to only sophomores until the number of high school students warranted another school. Approximately 95,000 square feet were added, and 26,000 square feet were remodeled to turn the South Campus into a totally separate high school. Thunder Basin High School opened with 1,072 students.

In 1981, the old hospital on Eighth Street closed, and the new hospital opened. In 1982, Northern Wyoming Community College president Dr. Gordon Ward signed an agreement with the hospital board to use the former emergency room and radiology areas as nurse-training classrooms. Additional areas of the former hospital were remodeled into classrooms later, and classes were held at any other available space. Today, Cottonwood Terrace Apartments flank the Campbell County Senior Center at that location.

This bridge sits on the ground waiting to be installed over Donkey Creek in December 2009. The bridge was heavier than expected and had to have floor planks and hand railings temporarily removed in order to cut back on weight enough that the crane could set it in place. In the present photograph, the bridge is out of sight to the right of the Gillette College Technical Center. The bridge joins the technical center with the first college building, "Old Main."

CHAPTER 7

Downtown Gillette, the Heart of Campbell County

Downtown is a great gauge of how prosperous a city is. This photograph of the second block of Gillette Avenue during a parade in the 1940s or 1950s shows a large crowd admiring the Eagles Lodge 2711 float. Two popular businesses, Ryan's Furniture and V-R Trading Post, are in the background.

The past picture shows a house that was part of the Gillette Avenue story for 107 years. Built in 1909 by William McCumiskey, a clothing merchant, this house was moved in early 2016 to property north of Rozet. Mike Cote, a Campbell County citizen, asked the owner, Christina Williams, if he could have the house if he moved it. Williams agreed, and Cote received a new renovation project. Williams built her new law office on that site.

In 1977, the coal industry in Campbell County was booming. One of the coal companies with a downtown Gillette office was Carter Mining Company. Carter Mining started in a smaller rock building at 510 South Gillette Avenue, currently the offices of Daly & Sorenson, LLC. In the present picture, the building's additions are apparent to the right of the older section. The last owner of the building was Cloud Peak Energy Company. The building is now owned by the county. (Past, courtesy of the City of Gillette.)

The Odd Fellows hall, shown in the past photograph, was built in 1919. It was the location for traveling road shows and dances from the 1920s to the 1950s. The 1930s were especially crowded, as the CCC boys flooded into town for their weekly fling. In 1921, the telephone company set up the switchboard on the second floor. The building was razed in 1978, when the current building was erected. State Farm insurance agent Ida Snead has been in this location since 2008. (Past, courtesy of the City of Gillette.)

The west side of Gillette Avenue looking south features several businesses in the past picture from the early 1960s that are also visible in the present picture in 2020. The Montgomery Bar and Hotel has been at this prominent corner location since 1911. The Center Bar, with its curved sign, has been on Gillette Avenue since 1941. The Fiesta Theatre burned in 1964, so obviously, the past photograph is from 1964 or before.

Look closely at the building on the far right in both photographs. The Stockman's Bank building looks similar today to how it looked in the 1940s and 1950s. This beautiful yellow brick building used to be in line with the Campbell County Chamber of Commerce and the Rodman Hotel. In the present picture, the small bank is dwarfed by the tallest building in Gillette, First Interstate Bank. The First Interstate Bank building was completed in 1959 as a one-story building.

Between 1981 and 1983, the First Interstate Bank building was expanded to seven stories tall. The old drive-up area on the west side of Warren Avenue was demolished, as shown in the past picture, and a more modern drive-up built behind the bank. The past picture shows the old Rodman Hotel to the left of the one-story bank. (Past, courtesy of First Interstate Bank.)

First National Bank opened on September 10, 1963, in a building north of the corner of Gillette Avenue and Fourth Street. At that time, Gillette's population was about 3,000. With plans to expand, a basement was dug just south of the original building. Unfortunately, the foundation wall of the old building caved into the newly dug basement, so the old building was torn down. The building in the past picture was built in 1969 and expanded to three stories in 1983. (Past, courtesy of the City of Gillette.)

In a land of limited resources, many buildings were moved in Campbell County rather than destroyed. This move in 1977 was captured on film. The building in the past photograph was originally near the county courthouse where the county commissioners wanted to provide parking space. Jim Slattery moved the house once used as a hospital to his land east of Gillette. The present picture shows Second Street today with the Frontier Auto Museum on the right and the Coop restaurant on the left.

In 1934, the Wyoming Hotel was at the southeast corner of Gillette Avenue and Third Street. The community wanted to build a post office on that corner, so the hotel was moved across the street to 316 South Gillette Avenue. The post office was built on the vacated corner and stands there today, although it is no longer a post office. The hotel became part of the building currently housing Consolidated Engineering. Notice the chimney in the present picture.

Harry Chassell is important in local history as the man who wrote the bill creating Campbell County out of parts of Crook and Weston Counties. His home was at the corner of Gillette Avenue and Seventh Street, but his business was Chassell & Fish, a general store at Gillette Avenue and Second Street, shown here around 1892. Ryan's Furniture, Gillette Commercial Company, and Teacher's Corner/Kid's Mart are other businesses that were here. Pain for Sale located here in June 2018.

Both icons in Gillette, the Dodd House was followed by the Goings. Both were hotels with a restaurant in a prominent location in the 100 block of Gillette Avenue. The Goings was sold to Ben Doud in December 1995. Former owners Georgia Lee and Danny Butler locked the door on the Goings on December 15. "It was the first time the door has ever been locked since it was built," said Georgia Lee. The stately Railyard restaurant continues here today.

Frank Olzer was a saddle maker by trade but also created gun belts, money clips, and saddlebags. He had a shop in Gillette in 1908. In 1918, he moved to Prescott, Arizona, and owned the Arizona Saddlery until 1936. Examples of his work are on display at the Campbell County Rockpile Museum and are still in use today. Fast forward to April 6, 2016, when Rapscallions Barbershop opened in a different building but the same location as Olzer's.

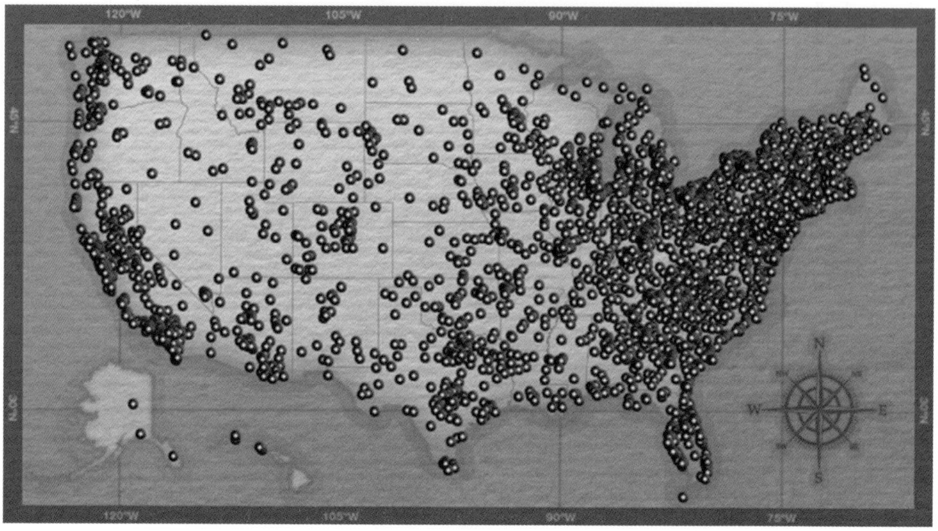